Cram101 Textbook Outlines to accompany:

An Applied Course in Real Options Valuation

Richard L. Shockley, 1st Edition

A Content Technologies Inc. publication (c) 2012.

STUDYING MADE EASY

This Craml0l notebook is designed to make studying easier and increase your comprehension of the textbook material. Instead of starting with a blank notebook and trying to write down everything discussed in class lectures, you can use this Craml0l textbook notebook and annotate your notes along with the lecture.

Our goal is to give you the best tools for success.

For a supreme understanding of the course, pair your notebook with our online tools. Should you decide you prefer Craml0l.com as your study tool,

we'd like to offer you a trade...

Our Trade In program is a simple way for us to keep our promise and provide you the best studying tools, regardless of where you purchased your Craml0l textbook notebook. As long as your notebook is in *Like New Condition**, you can send it back to us and we will immediately give you a Craml0l.com account free for 120 days!

Let The Trade In Begin!

THREE SIMPLE STEPS TO TRADE:

1. Go to www.cram101.com/tradein and fill out the packing slip information.

2. Submit and print the packing slip and mail it in with your Craml0l textbook notebook.

3. Activate your account after you receive your email confirmation.

* Books must be returned in *Like New Condition*, meaning there is no damage to the book including, but not limited to; ripped or torn pages, markings or writing on pages, or folded / creased pages. Upon receiving the book, Craml0l will inspect it and reserves the right to terminate your free Craml0l.com account and return your textbook notebook at the owners expense.

Learning System

Cram101 Textbook Outlines is a learning system. The notes in this book are the highlights of your textbook, you will never have to highlight a book again.

How to use this book. Take this book to class, it is your notebook for the lecture. The notes and highlights on the left hand side of the pages follow the outline and order of the textbook. All you have to do is follow along while your instructor presents the lecture. Circle the items emphasized in class and add other important information on the right side. With Cram101 Textbook Outlines you'll spend less time writing and more time listening. Learning becomes more efficient.

Cram101.com Online

Increase your studying efficiency by using Cram101.com's practice tests and online reference material. It is the perfect complement to Cram101 Textbook Outlines. Use self-teaching matching tests or simulate in-class testing with comprehensive multiple choice tests, or simply use Cram's true and false tests for quick review. Cram101.com even allows you to enter your in-class notes for an integrated studying format combining the textbook notes with your class notes.

Visit **www.Cram101.com**, click Sign Up at the top of the screen, and enter **DK73DW17578** in the promo code box on the registration screen. Your access to www.Cram101.com is discounted by 50% because you have purchased this book. Sign up and stop highlighting textbooks forever.

An Applied Course in Real Options Valuation
Richard L. Shockley, 1st

CONTENTS

Chapter 1. Motivation

Cash flow	Cash flow is the movement of cash into or out of a business, project, or financial product. (Note that "cash" is used here in the broader sense of the term, where it includes bank deposits). It is usually measured during a specified, finite period of time.
Investment	Investment is putting money into something with the expectation of profit. More specifically, investment is the commitment of money or capital to the purchase of financial instruments or other assets so as to gain profitable returns in the form of interest, income (dividends), or appreciation (capital gains) of the value of the instrument. It is related to saving or deferring consumption.
Stockholder	A mutual shareholder or Stockholder is an individual or company (including a corporation) that legally owns one or more shares of stock in a joint stock company. A company's shareholders collectively own that company. Thus, the typical goal of such companies is to enhance shareholder value.
Shareholder value	Shareholder value is a business buzz term, which implies that the ultimate measure of a company's success is to enrich shareholders. It became popular during the 1980s, and is particularly associated with former CEO of General Electric, Jack Welch. In March 2009, Welch criticized parts of the application of this concept, calling a focus on shareholder quarterly profit and share price gains "the dumbest idea in the world".
Asset	In financial accounting, assets are economic resources. Anything tangible or intangible that is capable of being owned or controlled to produce value and that is held to have positive economic value is considered an asset. Simply stated, assets represent ownership of value that can be converted into cash (although cash itself is also considered an asset).
Currency	In economics, currency refers to physical objects generally accepted as a medium of exchange. These are usually the coins and banknotes of a particular government, which comprise the physical aspects of a nation's money supply. The other part of a nation's money supply consists of bank deposits (sometimes called deposit money), ownership of which can be transferred by means of cheques, debit cards, or other forms of money transfer.
Currency risk	Currency risk is a form of risk that arises from the change in price of one currency against another. Whenever investors or companies have assets or business operations across national borders, they face currency risk if their positions are not hedged. • Transaction risk is the risk that exchange rates will change unfavourably over time.

Chapter 1. Motivation

Investment decisions	Investment decisions are made by investors and investment managers.
	Investors commonly perform investment analysis by making use of fundamental analysis, technical analysis and gut feel.
	Investment decisions are often supported by decision tools.
Present value	Present value is the value on a given date of a future payment or series of future payments, discounted to reflect the time value of money and other factors such as investment risk. Present value calculations are widely used in business and economics to provide a means to compare cash flows at different times on a meaningful "like to like" basis.
	If offered a choice between $100 today or $100 in one year and there is a positive real interest rate throughout the year ceteris paribus, a rational person will choose $100 today.
Specific risk	In finance, a specific risk is a risk that affects a very small number of assets. This is sometimes referred to as "unsystematic risk". In a balanced portfolio of assets there'd be a spread between general market risk and risks specific to individual components of that portfolio.
Financial market	In economics, a financial market is a mechanism that allows people to buy and sell (trade) financial securities (such as stocks and bonds), commodities (such as precious metals or agricultural goods), and other fungible items of value at low transaction costs and at prices that reflect the efficient-market hypothesis.
	Both general markets (where many commodities are traded) and specialized markets (where only one commodity is traded) exist. Markets work by placing many interested buyers and sellers in one "place", thus making it easier for them to find each other.
Market	•

Chapter 1. Motivation

A market is any one of a variety of systems, institutions, procedures, social relations and infrastructures whereby parties engage in exchange. While parties may exchange goods and services by barter, most markets rely on buyers offer their goods or services (including labor) in exchange for money (legal tender such as fiat money) from buyers.

For a market to be competitive, there must be more than a single buyer or seller.

Market value

Market value is the price at which an asset would trade in a competitive auction setting. Market value is often used interchangeably with open market value, fair value or fair market value, although these terms have distinct definitions in different standards, and may differ in some circumstances.

International Valuation Standards defines market value as "the estimated amount for which a property should exchange on the date of valuation between a willing buyer and a willing seller in an arm's-length transaction after proper marketing wherein the parties had each acted knowledgeably, prudently, and without compulsion."

Market value is a concept distinct from market price, which is "the price at which one can transact", while market value is "the true underlying value" according to theoretical standards.

Valuation

In finance, valuation is the process of estimating the potential market value of a financial asset or liability. Valuations can be done on assets (for example, investments in marketable securities such as stocks, options, business enterprises, or intangible assets such as patents and trademarks) or on liabilities (e.g., Bonds issued by a company). Valuations are required in many contexts including investment analysis, capital budgeting, merger and acquisition transactions, financial reporting, taxable events to determine the proper tax liability, and in litigation.

Binomial heap

In computer science, a binomial heap is a heap similar to a binary heap but also supports quickly merging two heaps. This is achieved by using a special tree structure. It is important as an implementation of the mergeable heap abstract data type (also called meldable heap), which is a priority queue supporting merge operation.

Chapter 1. Motivation

Investment strategy	In finance, an investment strategy is a set of rules, behaviors or procedures, designed to guide an investor's selection of an investment portfolio. Usually the strategy will be designed around the investor's risk-return tradeoff: some investors will prefer to maximize expected returns by investing in risky assets, others will prefer to minimize risk, but most will select a strategy somewhere in between. Passive strategies are often used to minimize transaction costs, and active strategies such as market timing are an attempt to maximize returns.
Free cash flow	In corporate finance, free cash flow is cash flow available for distribution among all the securities holders of an organization. They include equity holders, debt holders, preferred stock holders, convertible security holders, and so on. Note that the first three lines above are calculated for you on the standard Statement of Cash Flows.
Arbitrage	In economics and finance, arbitrage is the practice of taking advantage of a price difference between two or more markets: striking a combination of matching deals that capitalize upon the imbalance, the profit being the difference between the market prices. When used by academics, an arbitrage is a transaction that involves no negative cash flow at any probabilistic or temporal state and a positive cash flow in at least one state; in simple terms, it is the possibility of a risk-free profit at zero cost. In principle and in academic use, an arbitrage is risk-free; in common use, as in statistical arbitrage, it may refer to expected profit, though losses may occur, and in practice, there are always risks in arbitrage, some minor (such as fluctuation of prices decreasing profit margins), some major (such as devaluation of a currency or derivative).

Chapter 1. Motivation

Bond	In finance, a bond is a debt security, in which the authorized issuer owes the holders a debt and, depending on the terms of the bond, is obliged to pay interest (the coupon) and/or to repay the principal at a later date, termed maturity. A bond is a formal contract to repay borrowed money with interest at fixed intervals.
	Thus a bond is like a loan: the issuer is the borrower (debtor), the holder is the lender (creditor), and the coupon is the interest.
Pricing	Pricing is the process of determining what a company will receive in exchange for its products. Pricing factors are manufacturing cost, market place, competition, market condition, and quality of product. Pricing is also a key variable in microeconomic price allocation theory.
Decomposition	Decomposition is the process by which organic material is broken down into simpler forms of matter. The process is essential for recycling the finite matter that occupies physical space in the biome. Bodies of living organisms begin to decompose shortly after death.
Convenience	Convenience is anything that is intended to save resources (time, energy) or frustration. A convenience store at a petrol station, for example, sells items that have nothing to do with gasoline/petrol, but it saves the consumer from having to go to a grocery store. "Convenience" is a very relative term and its meaning tends to change over time.
Convenience yield	A convenience yield is an adjustment to the cost of carry in the non-arbitrage pricing formula for forward prices in markets with trading constraints.
	Let $F_{t,T}$ be the forward price of an asset with initial price S_t and maturity T. Suppose that r is the continuously compounded interest rate for one year.
Silicon Valley	Silicon Valley is in the southern part of the San Francisco Bay Area in Northern California in the United States. The region is home to many of the world's largest technology corporations. The term originally referred to the region's large number of silicon chip innovators and manufacturers, but eventually came to refer to all the high-tech businesses in the area; it is now generally used as a metonym for the American high-tech sector.

Clam101

Chapter 1. Motivation

Yield	In finance, the term yield describes the amount in cash that returns to the owners of a security. Normally it does not include the price variations, at the difference of the total return. Yield applies to various stated rates of return on stocks (common a).
Risk	Risk is the potential that a chosen action or activity (including the choice of inaction) will lead to a loss (an undesirable outcome). The notion implies that a choice having an influence on the outcome exists (or existed). Potential losses themselves may also be called "risks".
Capital asset	The term capital asset has three unrelated technical definitions, and is also used in a variety of non-technical ways. • In financial economics, it refers to any asset used to make money, as opposed to assets used for personal enjoyment or consumption. This is an important distinction because two people can disagree sharply about the value of personal assets, one person might think a sports car is more valuable than a pickup truck, another person might have the opposite taste.
Underlying	In finance, the underlying of a derivative is an asset, basket of assets, index, or even another derivative, such that the cash flows of the (former) derivative depend on the value of this underlying. There must be an independent way to observe this value to avoid conflicts of interest. According to the Financial Accounting Standards Board's FASB Statement of Financial Accounting Standards No. 133 (FAS 133) - Accounting for Derivative Instruments and Hedging Activities, an underlying is a specified interest rate, security price, commodity price, foreign exchange rate, index of prices or rates, or other variable (including the occurrence or nonoccurrence of a specified event such as a scheduled payment under a contract).
Income	Income is the consumption and savings opportunity gained by an entity within a specified time frame, which is generally expressed in monetary terms. However, for households and individuals, "income is the sum of all the wages, salaries, profits, interests payments, rents and other forms of earnings received... in a given period of time." For firms, income generally refers to net-profit: what remains of revenue after expenses have been subtracted. In the field of public economics, it may refer to the accumulation of both monetary and non-monetary consumption ability, the former being used as a proxy for total income.

Chapter 2. The Theory of Value

Arbitrage	In economics and finance, arbitrage is the practice of taking advantage of a price difference between two or more markets: striking a combination of matching deals that capitalize upon the imbalance, the profit being the difference between the market prices. When used by academics, an arbitrage is a transaction that involves no negative cash flow at any probabilistic or temporal state and a positive cash flow in at least one state; in simple terms, it is the possibility of a risk-free profit at zero cost. In principle and in academic use, an arbitrage is risk-free; in common use, as in statistical arbitrage, it may refer to expected profit, though losses may occur, and in practice, there are always risks in arbitrage, some minor (such as fluctuation of prices decreasing profit margins), some major (such as devaluation of a currency or derivative).
Option	In finance, an option is a derivative financial instrument that establishes a contract between two parties concerning the buying or selling of an asset at a reference price. The buyer of the option gains the right, but not the obligation, to engage in some specific transaction on the asset, while the seller incurs the obligation to fulfill the transaction if so requested by the buyer. Other types of options exist, and options can in principle be created for any type of valuable asset.
Valuation	In finance, valuation is the process of estimating the potential market value of a financial asset or liability. Valuations can be done on assets (for example, investments in marketable securities such as stocks, options, business enterprises, or intangible assets such as patents and trademarks) or on liabilities (e.g., Bonds issued by a company). Valuations are required in many contexts including investment analysis, capital budgeting, merger and acquisition transactions, financial reporting, taxable events to determine the proper tax liability, and in litigation.
Cash flow	Cash flow is the movement of cash into or out of a business, project, or financial product. (Note that "cash" is used here in the broader sense of the term, where it includes bank deposits). It is usually measured during a specified, finite period of time.
Financial market	In economics, a financial market is a mechanism that allows people to buy and sell (trade) financial securities (such as stocks and bonds), commodities (such as precious metals or agricultural goods), and other fungible items of value at low transaction costs and at prices that reflect the efficient-market hypothesis.

Chapter 2. The Theory of Value

Market	Both general markets (where many commodities are traded) and specialized markets (where only one commodity is traded) exist. Markets work by placing many interested buyers and sellers in one "place", thus making it easier for them to find each other. ● A market is any one of a variety of systems, institutions, procedures, social relations and infrastructures whereby parties engage in exchange. While parties may exchange goods and services by barter, most markets rely on buyers offer their goods or services (including labor) in exchange for money (legal tender such as fiat money) from buyers. For a market to be competitive, there must be more than a single buyer or seller.
Pricing	Pricing is the process of determining what a company will receive in exchange for its products. Pricing factors are manufacturing cost, market place, competition, market condition, and quality of product. Pricing is also a key variable in microeconomic price allocation theory.
Market risk	Market risk is the risk that the value of a portfolio, either an investment portfolio or a trading portfolio, will decrease due to the change in value of the market risk factors. The four standard market risk factors are stock prices, interest rates, foreign exchange rates, and commodity prices. The associated market risks are: ● Equity risk, the risk that stock prices and/or the implied volatility will change. ● Interest rate risk, the risk that interest rates and/or the implied volatility will change. ● Currency risk, the risk that foreign exchange rates and/or the implied volatility will change. ● Commodity risk, the risk that commodity prices (e.g. corn, copper, crude oil) and/or implied volatility will change. Measuring the potential loss amount due to market risk

Chapter 2. The Theory of Value

	As with other forms of risk, the potential loss amount due to market risk may be measured in a number of ways or conventions.
Asset	In financial accounting, assets are economic resources. Anything tangible or intangible that is capable of being owned or controlled to produce value and that is held to have positive economic value is considered an asset. Simply stated, assets represent ownership of value that can be converted into cash (although cash itself is also considered an asset).
Currency	In economics, currency refers to physical objects generally accepted as a medium of exchange. These are usually the coins and banknotes of a particular government, which comprise the physical aspects of a nation's money supply. The other part of a nation's money supply consists of bank deposits (sometimes called deposit money), ownership of which can be transferred by means of cheques, debit cards, or other forms of money transfer.
Currency risk	Currency risk is a form of risk that arises from the change in price of one currency against another. Whenever investors or companies have assets or business operations across national borders, they face currency risk if their positions are not hedged. • Transaction risk is the risk that exchange rates will change unfavourably over time.
Specific risk	In finance, a specific risk is a risk that affects a very small number of assets. This is sometimes referred to as "unsystematic risk". In a balanced portfolio of assets there'd be a spread between general market risk and risks specific to individual components of that portfolio.
Portfolio	In finance, a portfolio is a collection of investments held by an institution or an individual. Holding a portfolio is a part of an investment and risk-limiting strategy called diversification. By owning several assets, certain types of risk (in particular specific risk) can be reduced.
Market portfolio	Market portfolio is a portfolio consisting of a weighted sum of every asset in the market, with weights in the proportions that they exist in the market, with the necessary assumption that these assets are infinitely divisible.

Chapter 2. The Theory of Value

	Richard Roll's critique (1977) states that this is only a theoretical concept, as to create a market portfolio for investment purposes in practice would necessarily include every single possible available asset, including real estate, precious metals, stamp collections, jewelry, and anything with any worth, as the theoretical market being referred to would be the world market. As a result, proxies for the market are used in practice by investors.
Lottery Bond	Lottery Bonds are a type of government bond in which some randomly selected bonds within the issue are redeemed at a higher value than the face value of the bond.
	They are government bonds and only issued by a government. They have been issued by France, Belgium and the other major nations of Europe.
Bond	In finance, a bond is a debt security, in which the authorized issuer owes the holders a debt and, depending on the terms of the bond, is obliged to pay interest (the coupon) and/or to repay the principal at a later date, termed maturity. A bond is a formal contract to repay borrowed money with interest at fixed intervals.
	Thus a bond is like a loan: the issuer is the borrower (debtor), the holder is the lender (creditor), and the coupon is the interest.
Decomposition	Decomposition is the process by which organic material is broken down into simpler forms of matter. The process is essential for recycling the finite matter that occupies physical space in the biome. Bodies of living organisms begin to decompose shortly after death.
Index	In economics and finance, an index is a statistical measure of changes in a representative group of individual data points. These data may be derived from any number of sources, including company performance, prices, productivity, and employment. Economic indices track economic health from different perspectives.

Chapter 2. The Theory of Value

Risk-free bond	A risk-free bond is a theoretical bond that repays interest and principal with absolute certainty. The rate of return would be the risk-free interest rate. In practice, government bonds are treated as risk-free bonds, as governments can raise taxes or indeed print money to repay their domestic currency debt.
Government bond	A bond is a debt investment in which an investor loans a certain amount of money, for a certain amount of time, with a certain interest rate, to a company or country. A government bond is a bond issued by a national government denominated in the country's own currency. Bonds issued by national governments in foreign currencies are normally referred to as sovereign bonds.
Premium Bond	A Premium Bond is a lottery bond issued by the United Kingdom government's National Savings and Investments scheme. The government promises to buy back the bond, on request, for its original price. They were introduced by Harold Macmillan in his 1956 budget.
STOCK	The capital stock of a business entity represents the original capital paid into or invested in the business by its founders. It serves as a security for the creditors of a business since it cannot be withdrawn to the detriment of the creditors. Stock is distinct from the property and the assets of a business which may fluctuate in quantity and value.
Call option	A call option, often simply labeled a "call", is a financial contract between two parties, the buyer and the seller of this type of option. The buyer of the call option has the right, but not the obligation to buy an agreed quantity of a particular commodity or financial instrument (the underlying) from the seller of the option at a certain time (the expiration date) for a certain price (the strike price). The seller (or "writer") is obligated to sell the commodity or financial instrument should the buyer so decide.
Investment	Investment is putting money into something with the expectation of profit. More specifically, investment is the commitment of money or capital to the purchase of financial instruments or other assets so as to gain profitable returns in the form of interest, income (dividends), or appreciation (capital gains) of the value of the instrument. It is related to saving or deferring consumption.
Risk	Risk is the potential that a chosen action or activity (including the choice of inaction) will lead to a loss (an undesirable outcome). The notion implies that a choice having an influence on the outcome exists (or existed). Potential losses themselves may also be called "risks".

Chapter 2. The Theory of Value

Capital asset	The term capital asset has three unrelated technical definitions, and is also used in a variety of non-technical ways. • In financial economics, it refers to any asset used to make money, as opposed to assets used for personal enjoyment or consumption. This is an important distinction because two people can disagree sharply about the value of personal assets, one person might think a sports car is more valuable than a pickup truck, another person might have the opposite taste.
Underlying	In finance, the underlying of a derivative is an asset, basket of assets, index, or even another derivative, such that the cash flows of the (former) derivative depend on the value of this underlying. There must be an independent way to observe this value to avoid conflicts of interest. According to the Financial Accounting Standards Board's FASB Statement of Financial Accounting Standards No. 133 (FAS 133) - Accounting for Derivative Instruments and Hedging Activities, an underlying is a specified interest rate, security price, commodity price, foreign exchange rate, index of prices or rates, or other variable (including the occurrence or nonoccurrence of a specified event such as a scheduled payment under a contract).
Equity	In accounting and finance, equity is the residual claim or interest of the most junior class of investors in assets, after all liabilities are paid. If liability exceeds assets, negative equity exists. In an accounting context, Shareholders' equity represents the remaining interest in assets of a company, spread among individual shareholders of common or preferred stock.
Opportunity cost	Opportunity cost is the cost related to the next-best choice available to someone who has picked among several mutually exclusive choices. It is a key concept in economics. It has been described as expressing "the basic relationship between scarcity and choice." The notion of opportunity cost plays a crucial part in ensuring that scarce resources are used efficiently.
Price	In ordinary usage, price is the quantity of payment or compensation given by one party to another in return for goods or services.

Chapter 2. The Theory of Value

	In all modern economies, the overwhelming majority of prices are quoted in (and the transactions involve) units of some form of currency. Although in theory, prices could be quoted as quantities of other goods or services this sort of barter exchange is rarely seen.
Strike price	In options, the strike price is a key variable in a derivatives contract between two parties. Where the contract requires delivery of the underlying instrument, the trade will be at the strike price, regardless of the spot price (market price) of the underlying instrument at that time. Formally, the strike price can be defined as the fixed price at which the owner of an option can purchase (in the case of a call), or sell (in the case of a put), the underlying security or commodity.
Demand	In economics, demand is the desire to own anything, the ability to pay for it, and the willingness to pay . The term demand signifies the ability or the willingness to buy a particular commodity at a given point of time. Economists record demand on a demand schedule and plot it on a graph as a demand curve that is usually downward sloping.
Interest	Interest is a fee paid on borrowed assets. It is the price paid for the use of borrowed money, or, money earned by deposited funds. Assets that are sometimes lent with interest include money, shares, consumer goods through hire purchase, major assets such as aircraft, and even entire factories in finance lease arrangements.
Present value	Present value is the value on a given date of a future payment or series of future payments, discounted to reflect the time value of money and other factors such as investment risk. Present value calculations are widely used in business and economics to provide a means to compare cash flows at different times on a meaningful "like to like" basis.

Chapter 2. The Theory of Value

If offered a choice between $100 today or $100 in one year and there is a positive real interest rate throughout the year ceteris paribus, a rational person will choose $100 today.

Equity trading

In finance, equity trading is the buying and selling of company stock shares. Shares in large publicly-traded companies are bought and sold through one of the major stock exchanges, such as the New York Stock Exchange, London Stock Exchange or Tokyo Stock Exchange, which serve as managed auctions for stock trades. Stock shares in smaller public companies are bought and sold in over-the-counter (OTC) markets.

29

Chapter 3. The Binomial Mode

Option	In finance, an option is a derivative financial instrument that establishes a contract between two parties concerning the buying or selling of an asset at a reference price. The buyer of the option gains the right, but not the obligation, to engage in some specific transaction on the asset, while the seller incurs the obligation to fulfill the transaction if so requested by the buyer. Other types of options exist, and options can in principle be created for any type of valuable asset.
Distribution	Distribution in economics refers to the way total output, income, or wealth is distributed among individuals or among the factors of production (such as labour, land, and capital).. In general theory and the national income and product accounts, each unit of output corresponds to a unit of income. One use of national accounts is for classifying factor incomes and measuring their respective shares, as in National Income.
Investment	Investment is putting money into something with the expectation of profit. More specifically, investment is the commitment of money or capital to the purchase of financial instruments or other assets so as to gain profitable returns in the form of interest, income (dividends), or appreciation (capital gains) of the value of the instrument. It is related to saving or deferring consumption.
Asset	In financial accounting, assets are economic resources. Anything tangible or intangible that is capable of being owned or controlled to produce value and that is held to have positive economic value is considered an asset. Simply stated, assets represent ownership of value that can be converted into cash (although cash itself is also considered an asset).
Capital asset	The term capital asset has three unrelated technical definitions, and is also used in a variety of non-technical ways. • In financial economics, it refers to any asset used to make money, as opposed to assets used for personal enjoyment or consumption. This is an important distinction because two people can disagree sharply about the value of personal assets, one person might think a sports car is more valuable than a pickup truck, another person might have the opposite taste.
Underlying	In finance, the underlying of a derivative is an asset, basket of assets, index, or even another derivative, such that the cash flows of the (former) derivative depend on the value of this underlying. There must be an independent way to observe this value to avoid conflicts of interest.

Chapter 3. The Binomial Mode

According to the Financial Accounting Standards Board's FASB Statement of Financial Accounting Standards No. 133 (FAS 133) - Accounting for Derivative Instruments and Hedging Activities, an underlying is a specified interest rate, security price, commodity price, foreign exchange rate, index of prices or rates, or other variable (including the occurrence or nonoccurrence of a specified event such as a scheduled payment under a contract).

Present value	Present value is the value on a given date of a future payment or series of future payments, discounted to reflect the time value of money and other factors such as investment risk. Present value calculations are widely used in business and economics to provide a means to compare cash flows at different times on a meaningful "like to like" basis.
	If offered a choice between $100 today or $100 in one year and there is a positive real interest rate throughout the year ceteris paribus, a rational person will choose $100 today.
Pricing	Pricing is the process of determining what a company will receive in exchange for its products. Pricing factors are manufacturing cost, market place, competition, market condition, and quality of product. Pricing is also a key variable in microeconomic price allocation theory.
Arbitrage	In economics and finance, arbitrage is the practice of taking advantage of a price difference between two or more markets: striking a combination of matching deals that capitalize upon the imbalance, the profit being the difference between the market prices. When used by academics, an arbitrage is a transaction that involves no negative cash flow at any probabilistic or temporal state and a positive cash flow in at least one state; in simple terms, it is the possibility of a risk-free profit at zero cost.
	In principle and in academic use, an arbitrage is risk-free; in common use, as in statistical arbitrage, it may refer to expected profit, though losses may occur, and in practice, there are always risks in arbitrage, some minor (such as fluctuation of prices decreasing profit margins), some major (such as devaluation of a currency or derivative).

Chapter 3. The Binomial Mode

Valuation	In finance, valuation is the process of estimating the potential market value of a financial asset or liability. Valuations can be done on assets (for example, investments in marketable securities such as stocks, options, business enterprises, or intangible assets such as patents and trademarks) or on liabilities (e.g., Bonds issued by a company). Valuations are required in many contexts including investment analysis, capital budgeting, merger and acquisition transactions, financial reporting, taxable events to determine the proper tax liability, and in litigation.
Cash flow	Cash flow is the movement of cash into or out of a business, project, or financial product. (Note that "cash" is used here in the broader sense of the term, where it includes bank deposits). It is usually measured during a specified, finite period of time.
Portfolio	In finance, a portfolio is a collection of investments held by an institution or an individual.
	Holding a portfolio is a part of an investment and risk-limiting strategy called diversification. By owning several assets, certain types of risk (in particular specific risk) can be reduced.
Derivative	In finance, a derivative is a financial instrument (or, more simply, an agreement between two parties) that has a value, based on the expected future price movements of the asset to which it is linked--called the underlying asset-- such as a share or a currency. There are many kinds of derivatives, with the most common being swaps, futures, and options. Derivatives are a form of alternative investment.
Market	•
	A market is any one of a variety of systems, institutions, procedures, social relations and infrastructures whereby parties engage in exchange. While parties may exchange goods and services by barter, most markets rely on buyers offer their goods or services (including labor) in exchange for money (legal tender such as fiat money) from buyers.
	For a market to be competitive, there must be more than a single buyer or seller.

Chapter 3. The Binomial Mode

Index	In economics and finance, an index is a statistical measure of changes in a representative group of individual data points. These data may be derived from any number of sources, including company performance, prices, productivity, and employment. Economic indices track economic health from different perspectives.
Index fund	An index fund is a collective investment scheme (usually a mutual fund or exchange-traded fund) that aims to replicate the movements of an index of a specific financial market, or a set of rules of ownership that are held constant, regardless of market conditions. Tracking Tracking can be achieved by trying to hold all of the securities in the index, in the same proportions as the index. Other methods include statistically sampling the market and holding "representative" securities.
Risk theory	Risk theory connotes the study usually by actuaries and insurers of the financial impact on a carrier of a portfolio of insurance policies. For example, if the carrier has 100 policies that insures against a total loss of $1000, and if each policy's chance of loss is independent and has a probability of loss of p then the loss can be described by a binomial variable. With a large enough portfolio however, we can use the Poisson function for the frequency of loss variable where λ is used as the mean equal to the number of policies multiplied by p.
Currency	In economics, currency refers to physical objects generally accepted as a medium of exchange. These are usually the coins and banknotes of a particular government, which comprise the physical aspects of a nation's money supply. The other part of a nation's money supply consists of bank deposits (sometimes called deposit money), ownership of which can be transferred by means of cheques, debit cards, or other forms of money transfer.
Currency risk	Currency risk is a form of risk that arises from the change in price of one currency against another. Whenever investors or companies have assets or business operations across national borders, they face currency risk if their positions are not hedged. • Transaction risk is the risk that exchange rates will change unfavourably over time.

Chapter 3. The Binomial Mode

Specific risk	In finance, a specific risk is a risk that affects a very small number of assets. This is sometimes referred to as "unsystematic risk". In a balanced portfolio of assets there'd be a spread between general market risk and risks specific to individual components of that portfolio.
Marginal utility	In economics, the marginal utility of a good or service is the utility gained (or lost) from an increase (or decrease) in the consumption of that good or service. Economists sometimes speak of a law of diminishing marginal utility, meaning that the first unit of consumption of a good or service yields more utility than the second and subsequent units.
	The concept of marginal utility played a crucial role in the marginal revolution of the late 19th century, and led to the replacement of the labor theory of value by neoclassical value theory in which the relative prices of goods and services are simultaneously determined by marginal rates of substitution in consumption and marginal rates of transformation in production, which are equal in economic equilibrium.
Decomposition	Decomposition is the process by which organic material is broken down into simpler forms of matter. The process is essential for recycling the finite matter that occupies physical space in the biome. Bodies of living organisms begin to decompose shortly after death.
Binomial heap	In computer science, a binomial heap is a heap similar to a binary heap but also supports quickly merging two heaps. This is achieved by using a special tree structure. It is important as an implementation of the mergeable heap abstract data type (also called meldable heap), which is a priority queue supporting merge operation.
Model risk	In finance, model risk is the risk involved in using models to value financial securities. Rebonato considers alternative definitions including:

1. After observing a set of prices for the underlying and hedging instruments, different but identically calibrated models might produce different prices for the same exotic product.
2. Losses will be incurred because of an 'incorrect' hedging strategy suggested by a model.

Rebonato defines model risk as "the risk of occurrence of a significant difference between the mark-to-model value of a complex and/or illiquid instrument, and the price at which the same instrument is revealed to have traded in the market."

Types of model risk

Burke regards failure to use a model (instead over-relying on expert judgement) as a type of model risk. Derman describes various types of model risk that arise from using a model:

Wrong model

- Inapplicability of model.
- Incorrect model specification.

Model implementation

- Programming errors.
- Technical errors.
- Use of numerical approximations.

Model usage

- Implementation Risk.
- Data issues.
- Calibration errors.

Sources of model risk

Interest rate modelling

Buraschi and Corelli formalise the concept of 'time inconsistency' with regards to no-arbitrage models that allow for a perfect fit of the term structure of the interest rates.

Risk

Risk is the potential that a chosen action or activity (including the choice of inaction) will lead to a loss (an undesirable outcome). The notion implies that a choice having an influence on the outcome exists (or existed). Potential losses themselves may also be called "risks".

Chapter 3. The Binomial Mode

Silicon Valley	Silicon Valley is in the southern part of the San Francisco Bay Area in Northern California in the United States. The region is home to many of the world's largest technology corporations. The term originally referred to the region's large number of silicon chip innovators and manufacturers, but eventually came to refer to all the high-tech businesses in the area; it is now generally used as a metonym for the American high-tech sector.
STOCK	The capital stock of a business entity represents the original capital paid into or invested in the business by its founders. It serves as a security for the creditors of a business since it cannot be withdrawn to the detriment of the creditors. Stock is distinct from the property and the assets of a business which may fluctuate in quantity and value.
Investment decisions	Investment decisions are made by investors and investment managers. Investors commonly perform investment analysis by making use of fundamental analysis, technical analysis and gut feel. Investment decisions are often supported by decision tools.
Financial market	In economics, a financial market is a mechanism that allows people to buy and sell (trade) financial securities (such as stocks and bonds), commodities (such as precious metals or agricultural goods), and other fungible items of value at low transaction costs and at prices that reflect the efficient-market hypothesis. Both general markets (where many commodities are traded) and specialized markets (where only one commodity is traded) exist. Markets work by placing many interested buyers and sellers in one "place", thus making it easier for them to find each other.
Market value	Market value is the price at which an asset would trade in a competitive auction setting. Market value is often used interchangeably with open market value, fair value or fair market value, although these terms have distinct definitions in different standards, and may differ in some circumstances.

International Valuation Standards defines market value as "the estimated amount for which a property should exchange on the date of valuation between a willing buyer and a willing seller in an arm's-length transaction after proper marketing wherein the parties had each acted knowledgeably, prudently, and without compulsion."

Market value is a concept distinct from market price, which is "the price at which one can transact", while market value is "the true underlying value" according to theoretical standards.

Discounting	Discounting is a financial mechanism in which a debtor obtains the right to delay payments to a creditor, for a defined period of time, in exchange for a charge or fee. Essentially, the party that owes money in the present purchases the right to delay the payment until some future date. The discount, or charge, is simply the difference between the original amount owed in the present and the amount that has to be paid in the future to settle the debt.
Random variable	In probability and statistics, a random variable is a variable whose value results from a measurement on some random process. A random variable is a function, which maps events or outcomes (e.g., the possible results of rolling two dice: (1, 1), (1, 2), etc). to real numbers (e.g., their sum).
Binomial heap	In computer science, a binomial heap is a heap similar to a binary heap but also supports quickly merging two heaps. This is achieved by using a special tree structure. It is important as an implementation of the mergeable heap abstract data type (also called meldable heap), which is a priority queue supporting merge operation.

Chapter 4. European-Style Real Options

Binomial heap	In computer science, a binomial heap is a heap similar to a binary heap but also supports quickly merging two heaps. This is achieved by using a special tree structure. It is important as an implementation of the mergeable heap abstract data type (also called meldable heap), which is a priority queue supporting merge operation.
Investment	Investment is putting money into something with the expectation of profit. More specifically, investment is the commitment of money or capital to the purchase of financial instruments or other assets so as to gain profitable returns in the form of interest, income (dividends), or appreciation (capital gains) of the value of the instrument. It is related to saving or deferring consumption.
Investment strategy	In finance, an investment strategy is a set of rules, behaviors or procedures, designed to guide an investor's selection of an investment portfolio. Usually the strategy will be designed around the investor's risk-return tradeoff: some investors will prefer to maximize expected returns by investing in risky assets, others will prefer to minimize risk, but most will select a strategy somewhere in between.
	Passive strategies are often used to minimize transaction costs, and active strategies such as market timing are an attempt to maximize returns.
Market	•
	A market is any one of a variety of systems, institutions, procedures, social relations and infrastructures whereby parties engage in exchange. While parties may exchange goods and services by barter, most markets rely on buyers offer their goods or services (including labor) in exchange for money (legal tender such as fiat money) from buyers.
	For a market to be competitive, there must be more than a single buyer or seller.

Chapter 4. European-Style Real Options

Call option	A call option, often simply labeled a "call", is a financial contract between two parties, the buyer and the seller of this type of option. The buyer of the call option has the right, but not the obligation to buy an agreed quantity of a particular commodity or financial instrument (the underlying) from the seller of the option at a certain time (the expiration date) for a certain price (the strike price). The seller (or "writer") is obligated to sell the commodity or financial instrument should the buyer so decide.
Index	In economics and finance, an index is a statistical measure of changes in a representative group of individual data points. These data may be derived from any number of sources, including company performance, prices, productivity, and employment. Economic indices track economic health from different perspectives.
Option	In finance, an option is a derivative financial instrument that establishes a contract between two parties concerning the buying or selling of an asset at a reference price. The buyer of the option gains the right, but not the obligation, to engage in some specific transaction on the asset, while the seller incurs the obligation to fulfill the transaction if so requested by the buyer. Other types of options exist, and options can in principle be created for any type of valuable asset.
Valuation	In finance, valuation is the process of estimating the potential market value of a financial asset or liability. Valuations can be done on assets (for example, investments in marketable securities such as stocks, options, business enterprises, or intangible assets such as patents and trademarks) or on liabilities (e.g., Bonds issued by a company). Valuations are required in many contexts including investment analysis, capital budgeting, merger and acquisition transactions, financial reporting, taxable events to determine the proper tax liability, and in litigation.
Underlying	In finance, the underlying of a derivative is an asset, basket of assets, index, or even another derivative, such that the cash flows of the (former) derivative depend on the value of this underlying. There must be an independent way to observe this value to avoid conflicts of interest. According to the Financial Accounting Standards Board's FASB Statement of Financial Accounting Standards No. 133 (FAS 133) - Accounting for Derivative Instruments and Hedging Activities, an underlying is a specified interest rate, security price, commodity price, foreign exchange rate, index of prices or rates, or other variable (including the occurrence or nonoccurrence of a specified event such as a scheduled payment under a contract).

Chapter 4. European-Style Real Options

Asset	In financial accounting, assets are economic resources. Anything tangible or intangible that is capable of being owned or controlled to produce value and that is held to have positive economic value is considered an asset. Simply stated, assets represent ownership of value that can be converted into cash (although cash itself is also considered an asset).
Arbitrage	In economics and finance, arbitrage is the practice of taking advantage of a price difference between two or more markets: striking a combination of matching deals that capitalize upon the imbalance, the profit being the difference between the market prices. When used by academics, an arbitrage is a transaction that involves no negative cash flow at any probabilistic or temporal state and a positive cash flow in at least one state; in simple terms, it is the possibility of a risk-free profit at zero cost. In principle and in academic use, an arbitrage is risk-free; in common use, as in statistical arbitrage, it may refer to expected profit, though losses may occur, and in practice, there are always risks in arbitrage, some minor (such as fluctuation of prices decreasing profit margins), some major (such as devaluation of a currency or derivative).
Cash flow	Cash flow is the movement of cash into or out of a business, project, or financial product. (Note that "cash" is used here in the broader sense of the term, where it includes bank deposits). It is usually measured during a specified, finite period of time.
Volatility	In finance, volatility most frequently refers to the standard deviation of the continuously compounded returns of a financial instrument within a specific time horizon. It is common for discussions to talk about the volatility of a security's price, even while it is the returns' volatility that is being measured. It is used to quantify the risk of the financial instrument over the specified time period.
Pricing	Pricing is the process of determining what a company will receive in exchange for its products. Pricing factors are manufacturing cost, market place, competition, market condition, and quality of product. Pricing is also a key variable in microeconomic price allocation theory.
Break-even	Break-even is a point where any difference between plus or minus or equivalent changes side. In economics

In economics ' business, specifically cost accounting, the break-even point (BEP) is the point at which cost or expenses and revenue are equal: there is no net loss or gain, and one has "broken even". A profit or a loss has not been made, although opportunity costs have been paid, and capital has received the risk-adjusted, expected return.

Distribution

Distribution in economics refers to the way total output, income, or wealth is distributed among individuals or among the factors of production (such as labour, land, and capital).. In general theory and the national income and product accounts, each unit of output corresponds to a unit of income. One use of national accounts is for classifying factor incomes and measuring their respective shares, as in National Income.

Inflation

In economics, inflation is a rise in the general level of prices of goods and services in an economy over a period of time. When the general price level rises, each unit of currency buys fewer goods and services. Consequently, inflation also reflects an erosion in the purchasing power of money - a loss of real value in the internal medium of exchange and unit of account in the economy.

Market risk

Market risk is the risk that the value of a portfolio, either an investment portfolio or a trading portfolio, will decrease due to the change in value of the market risk factors. The four standard market risk factors are stock prices, interest rates, foreign exchange rates, and commodity prices. The associated market risks are:

- Equity risk, the risk that stock prices and/or the implied volatility will change.
- Interest rate risk, the risk that interest rates and/or the implied volatility will change.
- Currency risk, the risk that foreign exchange rates and/or the implied volatility will change.
- Commodity risk, the risk that commodity prices (e.g. corn, copper, crude oil) and/or implied volatility will change.

Measuring the potential loss amount due to market risk

As with other forms of risk, the potential loss amount due to market risk may be measured in a number of ways or conventions.

Chapter 4. European-Style Real Options

Currency	In economics, currency refers to physical objects generally accepted as a medium of exchange. These are usually the coins and banknotes of a particular government, which comprise the physical aspects of a nation's money supply. The other part of a nation's money supply consists of bank deposits (sometimes called deposit money), ownership of which can be transferred by means of cheques, debit cards, or other forms of money transfer.
Currency risk	Currency risk is a form of risk that arises from the change in price of one currency against another. Whenever investors or companies have assets or business operations across national borders, they face currency risk if their positions are not hedged. • Transaction risk is the risk that exchange rates will change unfavourably over time.
Risk	Risk is the potential that a chosen action or activity (including the choice of inaction) will lead to a loss (an undesirable outcome). The notion implies that a choice having an influence on the outcome exists (or existed). Potential losses themselves may also be called "risks".
Specific risk	In finance, a specific risk is a risk that affects a very small number of assets. This is sometimes referred to as "unsystematic risk". In a balanced portfolio of assets there'd be a spread between general market risk and risks specific to individual components of that portfolio.
Influence diagram	An influence diagram is a compact graphical and mathematical representation of a decision situation. It is a generalization of a Bayesian network, in which not only probabilistic inference problems but also decision making problems (following maximum expected utility criterion) can be modeled and solved.
Derivative	In finance, a derivative is a financial instrument (or, more simply, an agreement between two parties) that has a value, based on the expected future price movements of the asset to which it is linked--called the underlying asset-- such as a share or a currency. There are many kinds of derivatives, with the most common being swaps, futures, and options. Derivatives are a form of alternative investment.
Decomposition	Decomposition is the process by which organic material is broken down into simpler forms of matter. The process is essential for recycling the finite matter that occupies physical space in the biome. Bodies of living organisms begin to decompose shortly after death.

Chapter 5. American-Style Real Options

Derivative	In finance, a derivative is a financial instrument (or, more simply, an agreement between two parties) that has a value, based on the expected future price movements of the asset to which it is linked--called the underlying asset-- such as a share or a currency. There are many kinds of derivatives, with the most common being swaps, futures, and options. Derivatives are a form of alternative investment.
Investment	Investment is putting money into something with the expectation of profit. More specifically, investment is the commitment of money or capital to the purchase of financial instruments or other assets so as to gain profitable returns in the form of interest, income (dividends), or appreciation (capital gains) of the value of the instrument. It is related to saving or deferring consumption.
Option	In finance, an option is a derivative financial instrument that establishes a contract between two parties concerning the buying or selling of an asset at a reference price. The buyer of the option gains the right, but not the obligation, to engage in some specific transaction on the asset, while the seller incurs the obligation to fulfill the transaction if so requested by the buyer. Other types of options exist, and options can in principle be created for any type of valuable asset.
Asset	In financial accounting, assets are economic resources. Anything tangible or intangible that is capable of being owned or controlled to produce value and that is held to have positive economic value is considered an asset. Simply stated, assets represent ownership of value that can be converted into cash (although cash itself is also considered an asset).
Capital asset	The term capital asset has three unrelated technical definitions, and is also used in a variety of non-technical ways. • In financial economics, it refers to any asset used to make money, as opposed to assets used for personal enjoyment or consumption. This is an important distinction because two people can disagree sharply about the value of personal assets, one person might think a sports car is more valuable than a pickup truck, another person might have the opposite taste.
Underlying	In finance, the underlying of a derivative is an asset, basket of assets, index, or even another derivative, such that the cash flows of the (former) derivative depend on the value of this underlying. There must be an independent way to observe this value to avoid conflicts of interest.

Chapter 5. American-Style Real Options

According to the Financial Accounting Standards Board's FASB Statement of Financial Accounting Standards No. 133 (FAS 133) - Accounting for Derivative Instruments and Hedging Activities, an underlying is a specified interest rate, security price, commodity price, foreign exchange rate, index of prices or rates, or other variable (including the occurrence or nonoccurrence of a specified event such as a scheduled payment under a contract).

Pricing

Pricing is the process of determining what a company will receive in exchange for its products. Pricing factors are manufacturing cost, market place, competition, market condition, and quality of product. Pricing is also a key variable in microeconomic price allocation theory.

Income

Income is the consumption and savings opportunity gained by an entity within a specified time frame, which is generally expressed in monetary terms. However, for households and individuals, "income is the sum of all the wages, salaries, profits, interests payments, rents and other forms of earnings received... in a given period of time." For firms, income generally refers to net-profit: what remains of revenue after expenses have been subtracted. In the field of public economics, it may refer to the accumulation of both monetary and non-monetary consumption ability, the former being used as a proxy for total income.

Rate of return

In finance, rate of return also known as return on investment (ROI), rate of profit or sometimes just return, is the ratio of money gained or lost (whether realized or unrealized) on an investment relative to the amount of money invested. The amount of money gained or lost may be referred to as interest, profit/loss, gain/loss, or net income/loss. The money invested may be referred to as the asset, capital, principal, or the cost basis of the investment.

Returns

Returns, in economics and political economy, are the distributions or payments awarded to the various suppliers of the factors of production.

Wages

Wages are the return to labor--the return to an individual's involvement (mental or physical) in the creation or realization of goods or services. Wages are realized by an individual supplier of labor even if the supplier is the self.

CLAM101

Chapter 5. American-Style Real Options

Dividend	Dividends are payments made by a corporation to its shareholder members. It is the portion of corporate profits paid out to stockholders. When a corporation earns a profit or surplus, that money can be put to two uses: it can either be re-invested in the business (called retained earnings), or it can be paid to the shareholders as a dividend.
Call option	A call option, often simply labeled a "call", is a financial contract between two parties, the buyer and the seller of this type of option. The buyer of the call option has the right, but not the obligation to buy an agreed quantity of a particular commodity or financial instrument (the underlying) from the seller of the option at a certain time (the expiration date) for a certain price (the strike price). The seller (or "writer") is obligated to sell the commodity or financial instrument should the buyer so decide.
Index	In economics and finance, an index is a statistical measure of changes in a representative group of individual data points. These data may be derived from any number of sources, including company performance, prices, productivity, and employment. Economic indices track economic health from different perspectives.
Convenience	Convenience is anything that is intended to save resources (time, energy) or frustration. A convenience store at a petrol station, for example, sells items that have nothing to do with gasoline/petrol, but it saves the consumer from having to go to a grocery store. "Convenience" is a very relative term and its meaning tends to change over time.
Convenience yield	A convenience yield is an adjustment to the cost of carry in the non-arbitrage pricing formula for forward prices in markets with trading constraints. Let $F_{t,T}$ be the forward price of an asset with initial price S_t and maturity T. Suppose that r is the continuously compounded interest rate for one year.
Yield	In finance, the term yield describes the amount in cash that returns to the owners of a security. Normally it does not include the price variations, at the difference of the total return. Yield applies to various stated rates of return on stocks (common a).

Chapter 5. American-Style Real Options

Exercise	The owner of an option contract may exercise it, indicating that the financial transaction specified by the contract is to be enacted immediately between the two parties, and the contract itself is terminated. When exercising a call, the owner of the option purchases the underlying shares at the strike price from the option seller, while for a put, the owner of the option sells the underlying to the option seller. Exercise Type The option style determines when, how, and under what circumstances, the option holder may exercise.
Present value	Present value is the value on a given date of a future payment or series of future payments, discounted to reflect the time value of money and other factors such as investment risk. Present value calculations are widely used in business and economics to provide a means to compare cash flows at different times on a meaningful "like to like" basis. If offered a choice between $100 today or $100 in one year and there is a positive real interest rate throughout the year ceteris paribus, a rational person will choose $100 today.
Cash flow	Cash flow is the movement of cash into or out of a business, project, or financial product. (Note that "cash" is used here in the broader sense of the term, where it includes bank deposits). It is usually measured during a specified, finite period of time.
Valuation	In finance, valuation is the process of estimating the potential market value of a financial asset or liability. Valuations can be done on assets (for example, investments in marketable securities such as stocks, options, business enterprises, or intangible assets such as patents and trademarks) or on liabilities (e.g., Bonds issued by a company). Valuations are required in many contexts including investment analysis, capital budgeting, merger and acquisition transactions, financial reporting, taxable events to determine the proper tax liability, and in litigation.

Binomial heap	In computer science, a binomial heap is a heap similar to a binary heap but also supports quickly merging two heaps. This is achieved by using a special tree structure. It is important as an implementation of the mergeable heap abstract data type (also called meldable heap), which is a priority queue supporting merge operation.
Price	In ordinary usage, price is the quantity of payment or compensation given by one party to another in return for goods or services.
	In all modern economies, the overwhelming majority of prices are quoted in (and the transactions involve) units of some form of currency. Although in theory, prices could be quoted as quantities of other goods or services this sort of barter exchange is rarely seen.
Leverage	In finance, leverage is a general term for any technique to multiply gains and losses. Common ways to attain leverage are borrowing money, buying fixed assets and using derivatives. Important examples are:
	• A public corporation may leverage its equity by borrowing money.
Operating leverage	The operating leverage is a measure of how revenue growth translates into growth in operating income. It is a measure of leverage, and of how risky (volatile) a company's operating income is.
	There are various measures of operating leverage, which can be interpreted analogously to financial leverage.
Volatility	In finance, volatility most frequently refers to the standard deviation of the continuously compounded returns of a financial instrument within a specific time horizon. It is common for discussions to talk about the volatility of a security's price, even while it is the returns' volatility that is being measured. It is used to quantify the risk of the financial instrument over the specified time period.

Chapter 5. American-Style Real Options

Annuity	Annuity may refer to: • Annuity (distribution phase) any recurring payments • Life annuity: a financial contract providing payments for a person's lifetime • Annuity • Annuity An annuity that has no definite end is called a perpetuity.
Currency	In economics, currency refers to physical objects generally accepted as a medium of exchange. These are usually the coins and banknotes of a particular government, which comprise the physical aspects of a nation's money supply. The other part of a nation's money supply consists of bank deposits (sometimes called deposit money), ownership of which can be transferred by means of cheques, debit cards, or other forms of money transfer.
Currency risk	Currency risk is a form of risk that arises from the change in price of one currency against another. Whenever investors or companies have assets or business operations across national borders, they face currency risk if their positions are not hedged. • Transaction risk is the risk that exchange rates will change unfavourably over time.
Rainbow option	Rainbow option is a derivative exposed to two or more sources of uncertainty, as opposed to a simple option that is exposed to one source of uncertainty, such as the price of underlying asset. Rainbow options are usually calls or puts on the best or worst of n underlying assets, or options which pay the best or worst of n assets. The number of assets undelying the option is called the number of colours of the rainbow.
Arbitrage	In economics and finance, arbitrage is the practice of taking advantage of a price difference between two or more markets: striking a combination of matching deals that capitalize upon the imbalance, the profit being the difference between the market prices. When used by academics, an arbitrage is a transaction that involves no negative cash flow at any probabilistic or temporal state and a positive cash flow in at least one state; in simple terms, it is the possibility of a risk-free profit at zero cost.

	In principle and in academic use, an arbitrage is risk-free; in common use, as in statistical arbitrage, it may refer to expected profit, though losses may occur, and in practice, there are always risks in arbitrage, some minor (such as fluctuation of prices decreasing profit margins), some major (such as devaluation of a currency or derivative).
Financial market	In economics, a financial market is a mechanism that allows people to buy and sell (trade) financial securities (such as stocks and bonds), commodities (such as precious metals or agricultural goods), and other fungible items of value at low transaction costs and at prices that reflect the efficient-market hypothesis.
	Both general markets (where many commodities are traded) and specialized markets (where only one commodity is traded) exist. Markets work by placing many interested buyers and sellers in one "place", thus making it easier for them to find each other.
Market	•
	A market is any one of a variety of systems, institutions, procedures, social relations and infrastructures whereby parties engage in exchange. While parties may exchange goods and services by barter, most markets rely on buyers offer their goods or services (including labor) in exchange for money (legal tender such as fiat money) from buyers.
	For a market to be competitive, there must be more than a single buyer or seller.
STOCK	The capital stock of a business entity represents the original capital paid into or invested in the business by its founders. It serves as a security for the creditors of a business since it cannot be withdrawn to the detriment of the creditors. Stock is distinct from the property and the assets of a business which may fluctuate in quantity and value.

Chapter 5. American-Style Real Options

Petroleum	Petroleum is a naturally occurring, flammable liquid consisting of a complex mixture of hydrocarbons of various molecular weights and other liquid organic compounds, that are found in geologic formations beneath the Earth's surface. Petroleum is recovered mostly through oil drilling. It is refined and separated, most easily by boiling point, into a large number of consumer products, from gasoline and kerosene to asphalt and chemical reagents used to make plastics and pharmaceuticals.
Tax credit	A tax credit is a sum deducted from the total amount a taxpayer owes to the state. A tax credit may be granted for various types of taxes, such as an income tax, property tax, or VAT. It may be granted in recognition of taxes already paid, as a subsidy, or to encourage investment or other behaviors. In some systems tax credits are 'refundable' to the extent they exceed the relevant tax.
Credit	Credit is the trust which allows one party to provide resources to another party where that second party does not reimburse the first party immediately (thereby generating a debt), but instead arranges either to repay or return those resources (or other materials of equal value) at a later date. The resources provided may be financial (e.g. granting a loan), or they may consist of goods or services (e.g. consumer credit). Credit encompasses any form of deferred payment.
Inflation	In economics, inflation is a rise in the general level of prices of goods and services in an economy over a period of time. When the general price level rises, each unit of currency buys fewer goods and services. Consequently, inflation also reflects an erosion in the purchasing power of money - a loss of real value in the internal medium of exchange and unit of account in the economy.
Strike price	In options, the strike price is a key variable in a derivatives contract between two parties. Where the contract requires delivery of the underlying instrument, the trade will be at the strike price, regardless of the spot price (market price) of the underlying instrument at that time.
	Formally, the strike price can be defined as the fixed price at which the owner of an option can purchase (in the case of a call), or sell (in the case of a put), the underlying security or commodity.

Cost	In business, retail, and accounting, a cost is the value of money that has been used up to produce something, and hence is not available for use anymore. In economics, a cost is an alternative that is given up as a result of a decision. In business, the cost may be one of acquisition, in which case the amount of money expended to acquire it is counted as cost.
Specific risk	In finance, a specific risk is a risk that affects a very small number of assets. This is sometimes referred to as "unsystematic risk". In a balanced portfolio of assets there'd be a spread between general market risk and risks specific to individual components of that portfolio.
Spot price	The spot price, a security or a currency is the price that is quoted for immediate (spot) settlement (payment and delivery). Spot settlement is normally one or two business days from trade date. This is in contrast with the forward price established in a forward contract or futures contract, where contract terms (price) are set now, but delivery and payment will occur at a future date.

Chapter 6. Conclusion

Lattice model	In finance, a lattice model can be used to find the fair value of a stock option; variants also exist for interest rate derivatives. The model divides time between now and the option's expiration into N discrete periods. At the specific time n, the model has an infinite number of outcomes at time n + 1 such that every possible change in the state of the world between n and n + 1 is captured in a branch.
Simulation	Simulation is the imitation of some real thing, state of affairs, or process. The act of simulating something generally entails representing certain key characteristics or behaviours of a selected physical or abstract system. Simulation is used in many contexts, such as simulation of technology for performance optimization, safety engineering, testing, training, education, and video games.
Risk-free bond	A risk-free bond is a theoretical bond that repays interest and principal with absolute certainty. The rate of return would be the risk-free interest rate. In practice, government bonds are treated as risk-free bonds, as governments can raise taxes or indeed print money to repay their domestic currency debt.
Cash flow	Cash flow is the movement of cash into or out of a business, project, or financial product. (Note that "cash" is used here in the broader sense of the term, where it includes bank deposits). It is usually measured during a specified, finite period of time.
STOCK	The capital stock of a business entity represents the original capital paid into or invested in the business by its founders. It serves as a security for the creditors of a business since it cannot be withdrawn to the detriment of the creditors. Stock is distinct from the property and the assets of a business which may fluctuate in quantity and value.
Index	In economics and finance, an index is a statistical measure of changes in a representative group of individual data points. These data may be derived from any number of sources, including company performance, prices, productivity, and employment. Economic indices track economic health from different perspectives.
Option	In finance, an option is a derivative financial instrument that establishes a contract between two parties concerning the buying or selling of an asset at a reference price. The buyer of the option gains the right, but not the obligation, to engage in some specific transaction on the asset, while the seller incurs the obligation to fulfill the transaction if so requested by the buyer. Other types of options exist, and options can in principle be created for any type of valuable asset.

Chapter 6. Conclusion

Portfolio	In finance, a portfolio is a collection of investments held by an institution or an individual. Holding a portfolio is a part of an investment and risk-limiting strategy called diversification. By owning several assets, certain types of risk (in particular specific risk) can be reduced.
Asset	In financial accounting, assets are economic resources. Anything tangible or intangible that is capable of being owned or controlled to produce value and that is held to have positive economic value is considered an asset. Simply stated, assets represent ownership of value that can be converted into cash (although cash itself is also considered an asset).
Investment	Investment is putting money into something with the expectation of profit. More specifically, investment is the commitment of money or capital to the purchase of financial instruments or other assets so as to gain profitable returns in the form of interest, income (dividends), or appreciation (capital gains) of the value of the instrument. It is related to saving or deferring consumption.
Pricing	Pricing is the process of determining what a company will receive in exchange for its products. Pricing factors are manufacturing cost, market place, competition, market condition, and quality of product. Pricing is also a key variable in microeconomic price allocation theory.
Arbitrage	In economics and finance, arbitrage is the practice of taking advantage of a price difference between two or more markets: striking a combination of matching deals that capitalize upon the imbalance, the profit being the difference between the market prices. When used by academics, an arbitrage is a transaction that involves no negative cash flow at any probabilistic or temporal state and a positive cash flow in at least one state; in simple terms, it is the possibility of a risk-free profit at zero cost. In principle and in academic use, an arbitrage is risk-free; in common use, as in statistical arbitrage, it may refer to expected profit, though losses may occur, and in practice, there are always risks in arbitrage, some minor (such as fluctuation of prices decreasing profit margins), some major (such as devaluation of a currency or derivative).

Chapter 6. Conclusion

Binomial heap	In computer science, a binomial heap is a heap similar to a binary heap but also supports quickly merging two heaps. This is achieved by using a special tree structure. It is important as an implementation of the mergeable heap abstract data type (also called meldable heap), which is a priority queue supporting merge operation.
Capital asset	The term capital asset has three unrelated technical definitions, and is also used in a variety of non-technical ways.

- In financial economics, it refers to any asset used to make money, as opposed to assets used for personal enjoyment or consumption. This is an important distinction because two people can disagree sharply about the value of personal assets, one person might think a sports car is more valuable than a pickup truck, another person might have the opposite taste. |
| Decomposition | Decomposition is the process by which organic material is broken down into simpler forms of matter. The process is essential for recycling the finite matter that occupies physical space in the biome. Bodies of living organisms begin to decompose shortly after death. |
| Underlying | In finance, the underlying of a derivative is an asset, basket of assets, index, or even another derivative, such that the cash flows of the (former) derivative depend on the value of this underlying. There must be an independent way to observe this value to avoid conflicts of interest.

According to the Financial Accounting Standards Board's FASB Statement of Financial Accounting Standards No. 133 (FAS 133) - Accounting for Derivative Instruments and Hedging Activities, an underlying is a specified interest rate, security price, commodity price, foreign exchange rate, index of prices or rates, or other variable (including the occurrence or nonoccurrence of a specified event such as a scheduled payment under a contract). |

Chapter 6. Conclusion

Valuation	In finance, valuation is the process of estimating the potential market value of a financial asset or liability. Valuations can be done on assets (for example, investments in marketable securities such as stocks, options, business enterprises, or intangible assets such as patents and trademarks) or on liabilities (e.g., Bonds issued by a company). Valuations are required in many contexts including investment analysis, capital budgeting, merger and acquisition transactions, financial reporting, taxable events to determine the proper tax liability, and in litigation.
Present value	Present value is the value on a given date of a future payment or series of future payments, discounted to reflect the time value of money and other factors such as investment risk. Present value calculations are widely used in business and economics to provide a means to compare cash flows at different times on a meaningful "like to like" basis.
	If offered a choice between $100 today or $100 in one year and there is a positive real interest rate throughout the year ceteris paribus, a rational person will choose $100 today.
Market	•
	A market is any one of a variety of systems, institutions, procedures, social relations and infrastructures whereby parties engage in exchange. While parties may exchange goods and services by barter, most markets rely on buyers offer their goods or services (including labor) in exchange for money (legal tender such as fiat money) from buyers.
	For a market to be competitive, there must be more than a single buyer or seller.
Market portfolio	Market portfolio is a portfolio consisting of a weighted sum of every asset in the market, with weights in the proportions that they exist in the market, with the necessary assumption that these assets are infinitely divisible.

Chapter 6. Conclusion

Richard Roll's critique (1977) states that this is only a theoretical concept, as to create a market portfolio for investment purposes in practice would necessarily include every single possible available asset, including real estate, precious metals, stamp collections, jewelry, and anything with any worth, as the theoretical market being referred to would be the world market. As a result, proxies for the market are used in practice by investors.

9 781428 809680